The Perfect Blend

Drinkmaker's Guide

Compiled by
Nancy L. Lockhart

Illustrations and cover design by
Brian Santos

Cover Photography by
Arthur Lee

D0168064

Enterprise Publication
Copyright 1984
All Rights Reserved
0-914883-003 ISBN
Printed in U.S.A.

TABLE OF CONTENTS

Page

BAR DRINKS (Containing Alcohol)

TABLE OF CONTENTS (Continued)

PUNCHES (Containing Alcohol)

TABLE OF CONTENTS (Continued)

NON-ALCOHOLIC DRINKS

TABLE OF CONTENTS (Continued)

PUNCHES (Non-Alcoholic)

INTRODUCTION

CNL Enterprise Publications proudly introduces the first complete, versatile, drink book for use at home.

Here, in one convenient easy to read volume, are more than 200 of the most popular drinks requested in fine bars and restaurants. In addition there are assorted alcoholic party punches, individual hot cocktails and a section containing numerous non-alcoholic drinks and punches, so you can toast in the New Year, and continue throughout the seasons with a festive array of good tasting, creative alternatives to alcoholic beverages. There are yummy shakes and ice cream floats for an anytime snack, flavorful vegetable cocktails to serve before an elegant dinner and enough creative concoctions to keep your party punch bowl popular.

Included too is advice on everything you'll need to stock your own bar.

The recipes contained here have been carefully selected, authenticated and tested to give you the confidence you need for successful at home entertaining.

When you consult the Perfect Blend Drink-maker's Guide you will find its clear everyday language and easy to make recipes are like having a professional party consultant right at your elbow.

When unexpected family or friends drop in, when special party occasions arise, or when someone just wants something good to drink, you will find this book a valuable addition to your reference recipe bookshelf and a gift that any party giver would be grateful to receive.

Bar Drinks (Containing Alcohol)

ANGEL'S TIP

Use Pousse-Café glass or cordial glass
¾ ounce brown or white Creme De Cacao
¼ ounce cream

Float cream and spear maraschino cherry with a toothpick and place on top.

AMARETTO COBBLER

12 ounce glass filled with crushed ice
1½ ounces gin
2 ounces orange juice
1 ounce lemon juice
½ ounce Amaretto

Mix, add more ice to fill glass to top, stir. Add orange slice as garnish

BATTERING RAM

14 ounce glass, ½ full of ice
Mixing cup with 4 ounces ice
1 ounce light rum
1 ounce dark rum
4 ounces orange juice
½ ounce Wild Turkey liquor
½ ounce lime juice

Mix, strain into 14 ounce glass. Fill glass with tonic water. Add slice of lime.

BLOODY MARY

Highball glass - 12 ounce
1 ounce vodka
3 ounces tomato juice
1 teaspoon lemon juice
½ teaspoon Worcestershire sauce
2 drops tabasco sauce

Shake with ice and strain into highball glass filled with ice cubes. Garnish with stalk of celery and wedge of lime.

Editor's Note: For spicier Bloody Mary substitute V-8 juice for tomato juice.

BACARDI

1 ounce Bacardi Rum
½ ounce Grenadine
Juice of 1/2 lime

Shake with ice and strain into cocktail glass.

B & B

Cordial glass
½ ounce benedictine
½ ounce brandy

Carefully float brandy over the benedictine by pouring brandy over the back of a spoon.

BANSHEE

Cocktail glass - 5½ ounce
1 ounce Creme De Banana
1 ounce white Creme De Cacao
1 ounce cream

Shake with ice and strain.

BETWEEN THE SHEETS

Cocktail glass - 5½ ounce
¾ ounce light rum
¾ ounce brandy
¾ ounce triple sec

Shake with ice and strain into cocktail glass.

BLUE DEVIL

Cocktail or Tulip glass - 5½ ounce
1½ ounce gin
½ ounce Blue Curacao
½ ounce lemon juice
1 slice of lime

Blend gin, Curacao with ice. Strain. Garnish with wedge of lime.

BLUE ANGEL

Cocktail or Tulip glass - 5½ ounce
½ ounce Blue Curacao
½ ounce brandy
½ ounce white Creme De Cacao
½ ounce lime juice
½ ounce cream

Shake well with ice. Strain into cocktail glass.

BLUE HAWAIIAN PUNCH

Tulip glass - 5½ ounce
2 ounces lemon juice
1 ounce pineapple juice
1 ounce light rum
½ ounce Blue Curacao
Ice

Mix in blender 15 seconds. Garnish with slice of pineapple.

BLACK RUSSIAN

Cocktail glass · 5 ounce
1 ounce vodka
1 ounce Kahlua

Pour over ice cubes into cocktail glass.

BLACK MEXICAN (OR BRAVE BULL)

Cocktail glass · 5 ounce
1 ounce tequila
1 ounce Kahlua

Pour over ice cubes into cocktail glass.

BLOODY MARIA

1 ounce tequila
2 ounces tomato juice
1 teaspoon lime juice
1 dash tabasco sauce
1 dash celery salt

Mix all ingredients with cracked ice. Strain into highball glass over ice cubes — garnish with slice of lime.

Editor's Note: For spicier Bloody Maria substitute V-8 juice for tomato juice.

BEER BUSTER

Beer Mug
1½ ounce cold vodka
2 dashes of tabasco sauce

Fill with beer; stir gently.

BRANDY ALEXANDER

Cocktail glass - 5½ ounce
½ ounce white Creme De Cacao
½ ounce brandy
2 ounces cream

Shake with ice, strain into cocktail glass.

BOCCIE BALL

Highball glass - 5½ ounce
1 ounce Amaretto
2 ounces orange juice
2 ounces club soda

Mix, serve in a highball glass over ice.

BULL SHOT

4 ounces chilled beef bouillon
1½ ounces vodka
1 dash Worcestershire sauce
1 dash salt

Shake with cracked ice and strain into highball glass. Garnish with lemon slice.

CAPE CODDER

8 oz. highball glass ½ full ice
1½ ounces vodka
Cranberry juice

Fill balance of glass with cranberry juice. Garnish with slice of lime.

CAPPUCCINO (HOT) COCKTAIL

½ ounce coffee flavored brandy
½ ounce vodka
7 ounces hot milk

Mix. Pour into a tumbler.

CHAMPAGNE COCKTAIL

Champagne glass - 3½ ounce
1 lump sugar
1 dash bitters

Place in champagne glass and fill with chilled champagne. Add a twist of lemon peel.

CHAMPAGNE PUNCH

2 bottles pink champagne
¼ pound sugar
1 quart 7-Up
2 quarts club soda
1 pint brandy
8 ounces triple sec
1 quart orange juice

Mix in punch bowl over block of ice.

COFFEE COCKTAIL

1 whole egg
1 teaspoon powdered sugar
1 ounce port wine
1 ounce coffee flavored brandy

Shake with ice and strain into glass.

COFFEE (HOT) COCKTAIL

1 teaspoon sugar
1 ounce brandy

Pour into mug, fill up with hot black coffee.

Optional — Place 1 ounce cream in cup before adding coffee.

CUBA LIBRE OR (RUM AND COLA)

14 ounce collins glass ½ with ice
2 ounces light rum
½ lime

Fill with cola.

DAIQUIRI

Cocktail glass - 6 ounce
Mixing cup 4 ounces ice
½ ounce sweet lemon juice
1 ounce rum

Blend 20 seconds and pour.

DEVIL'S DELIGHT

Cocktail glass - 5½ ounce
Mixing cup 4 ounces ice
1½ ounces orange juice
1 ounce Amaretto
½ ounce cream

Blend 20 seconds and strain.

DIRTY MOTHER

5½ ounce Manhattan glass ½ full ice
1 ounce brandy
1 ounce Kahlua
1 ounce cream

Mix and Serve.

DRY MANHATTAN

Manhattan glass · 5½ ounce
Fill glass ¾ ice
1½ ounces whiskey
¼ ounce dry vermouth

One olive on spear.

DUBONNET COCKTAIL

Cocktail glass 3½ ounce
1¼ ounces Dubonnet wine
1¼ ounces gin

Stir well in ice and strain into glass. Garnish with lemon peel.

FLAMING IRISH COFFEE

8 ounce cup
Fill 3/4 with hot coffee
¾ ounce Irish whiskey on top of coffee

In a teaspoon mix ½ teaspoon sugar saturated with Irish whiskey. Place contents in spoon over flame, ignite. Hold ignited spoon to top of coffee to create flame in cup.

FRENCH TICKLER (OR FRENCH KISS)

Stemmed glass · 4½ ounce
2 ounces sweet vermouth
2 ounces dry vermouth

Pour over ice in glass. Rim glass with lemon peel, drop peel into glass.

FRENCH 69

Collins glass · 11 ounce
Mixing cup 5 ounces ice
2 ounces sweet lemon juice
1 ounce gin

Blend. Top off glass with champagne.

FROZEN DAIQUIRI

Cocktail glass · 6 ounce
Mixing Cup 5 ounces ice
2 ounces sweet lemon juice
1 ounce light rum
½ ounce triple sec

Blend 2 minutes. Spoon into glass, mound up and place same size glass over mound to shape. Garnish with maraschino cherry. Stand, strain in glass.

FROZEN FRUIT DAIQUIRIS

Pre-chilled deep saucer champagne glass
1½ ounces light rum
½ ounce lime juice
1 teaspoon sugar
½ cup crushed ice

Blend low speed 10-15 seconds. To create fruit daiquiris add:
1 ounce fruit nectar or syrup
1 ounce fruit juice or liqueur

GIMLET

Pre-chilled Manhattan glass · 4½ ounce
½ ounce Rose's lime juice
1½ ounces gin

Stir in glass to chill. Strain and pour. Garnish with slice of lime.

GIN AND TONIC

Highball glass · 8 ounce
Fill with ice
1½ ounces gin

Fill with tonic. Squeeze slice of lime into glass. Put lime into glass.

GIN BUCK

Highball glass · 12 ounce
Juice of ½ lemon or ½ ounce sweet lemon juice
1½ ounces gin

Fill glass with ginger ale. Mix and serve.

GIN PRESBYTERIAN

Highball glass · 8 ounce
Fill with ice
1 ounce gin

Fill halfway with ginger ale and complete with soda.
Substitute any other liquor desired for gin.

GODFATHER

Manhattan glass · 5 ounce
Fill ¾ with ice
1½ ounces Scotch
½ ounce Amaretto

GOLD CADILLAC

Pre-chilled champagne glass
¾ ounce Creme De Cacao
¾ ounce Galliano
¾ ounce cream
⅓ cup crushed ice

Blend low speed for 15 seconds. Strain into champagne glass.

GRASSHOPPER

Pre-chilled champagne glass · 4½ ounce
¾ ounce white Creme De Cacao
¾ ounce Green Creme De Menthe
¾ ounce cream

Shake well with ice and strain into pre-chilled champagne glass.

GRASS SKIRT

Large cocktail glass · 4½ ounce
1 ounce Coco Ribe
½ ounce rum
1 ounce pineapple juice
½ lime juice

Shake well with ice. Pour into pre-chilled cocktail glass with sugar frosted rim.

GIN ALEXANDER

Cocktail Glass 5½ ounces
½ ounce white Creme De Cacao
½ ounce gin
2 ounces cream

Shake with ice, strain into cocktail glass.

HARVEY WALLBANGER

Highball glass · 8 ounce
1½ ounces vodka
4½ ounces orange juice
¾ ounce Galliano

Mix, pour over rocks into highball glass

HOT BUTTERED RUM

Coffee mug
1 ounce rum
1 lump of sugar or 1 teaspoon sugar
Fill with hot water
Add 1 slice butter
Top with whipped cream
Sprinkle with nutmeg or cinnamon

HOT TODDY

Coffee mug
1 lump sugar
2 ounces brandy
Fill with hot water and stir
1 slice lemon
1 stick of cinnamon

IRISH COFFEE

Coffee Mug
½ ounce simple syrup
1 ounce Irish mist
Fill with hot coffee
Top with whipped cream
Sprinkle with nutmeg

JOHN COLLINS

Collins glass · 11 ounces
Fill glass ¾ with ice
2½ ounces lemon juice
1 ounce Dutch Genever Gin
Fill to top with soda
Garnish with lemon slice

MAI-TAI

Double old fashioned glass - 15 ounce
Mixing cup ½ filled with ice
1 ounce lime juice
1 tablespoon of Orgeat or Almond
  flavored syrup
1 ounce triple sec
2 ounces light rum

Blend and pour. Garnish with maraschino cherry and slice of lime.

MANHATTAN

Manhattan glass - 4½ ounce
Fill glass ¾ with ice
1½ ounces whiskey
½ ounce sweet vermouth
Mix, garnish with cherry and serve.

MARGARITA

Cocktail glass - 9 ounce
1½ ounces tequila
½ ounce triple sec
½ ounce lemon or lime juice

Shake well with ice; strain and pour into pre-chilled salt rimmed glass. Garnish with slice of lime.
To salt glass rim — rub with lemon peel, dip in salt and shake off excess.

MARTINI

Cocktail glass · 3½ ounce
Mixing cup 5 ounces ice
2 ounces gin
1 teaspoon dry vermouth

Shake contents in ice. Strain into pre-chilled glass. Add olive on spear.

MINT JULEP

Collins glass · Shaved ice · 11 ounce
2½ ounces bourbon
5 or 6 mint leaves muddled
1 teaspoon sugar
2½ ounces water

Stir until ice melts. Add more ice to fill glass. Garnish with mint.

MOSCOW MULE

Tall 12 to 14 oz. glass, ½ filled with ice
1½ ounces vodka
Juice of ½ lime

Fill glass with iced ginger beer. Garnish with slice of lime.

OLD FASHIONED

Old Fashioned glass · 7 ounce
Fill with ice
½ teaspoon sugar
1 dash bitters
1½ ounces whiskey
Dash soda

Add twist of lemon peel. Garnish with cherry.

ORANGE BLOSSOM

Cocktail glass · 4½ ounce
1 ounce gin
1 ounce orange juice

Shake with ice, strain, pour into pre-chilled glass.

PERFECT MANHATTAN

Pre-chilled Manhattan glass · 5 ounce
Fill glass ¾ ice
½ ounce dry vermouth
½ ounce sweet vermouth
1½ ounce whiskey

Garnish with lemon twist and drop peel into drink.

PINA COLADA

Pre-chilled glass - 8 ounce
1 ½ ounce light rum
1 ounce coconut milk
3 ounces pineapple juice

Pour into blender with 3 ice cubes; blend 20 seconds until ice crushed. Pour over rocks. Stir and serve.

PINK SQUIRREL COCKTAIL

Cocktail glass · 5½ ounce
1 ounce Creme De Noyaux or Creme De Almond
1 ounce Creme De Cacao (white)
¾ ounce cream

Blend with ice, strain. Pour into pre-chilled cocktail glass.

PINK LADY

Cocktail glass · 6 ounce
1½ ounces gin
1 teaspoon lime juice
1 teaspoon cream
1 teaspoon Grenadine
1 egg white

Shake well with ice. Strain — pour into pre-chilled cocktail glass.

PLANTERS PUNCH

Collins glass · 11 ounce
Mixing cup, ice
1 ounce lemon juice
1 dash bitters
½ ounce Grenadine
1½ ounce dark rum

Blend and pour; fill with soda. Garnish with speared maraschino cherry.

POUSSE CAFE

Cordial glass
Pour in this exact order
equal parts of:
White Creme De Menthe
Green Creme De Menthe
Banana Liqueur
Cherry Heering
Tuaca
Top with light cream

RAMOS FIZZ

Collins glass · 11 ounce
2 ounces lemon juice
½ ounce cream
1 ounce gin
2 dashes orange flower water
1 egg white

Fill with soda; blend and pour.

RABBITS FOOT

5½ ounce glass pre-chilled
¾ ounce Applejack
¾ ounce light rum
½ ounce orange juice
½ ounce lemon juice
¼ ounce Grenadine

Shake with ice; strain. Garnish with orange slice.

ROB ROY

5 ounce glass
Fill with ice
1 ounce Scotch
¼ ounce sweet vermouth
1 dash bitters

Garnish with speared olive.

RUM COOLER

14 ounce glass
Mixing cup - 4 ounces ice
2½ ounces light rum
1 ounce Creme De Coconut
½ ounce lemon juice

Blend and strain. Garnish with orange slice and cherry.

RUM AND COKE

8 ounce glass filled with ice
1 ounce rum
Fill with Coke

RUSTY NAIL

5½ ounce glass, ice
¾ ounce Scotch
¾ ounce Drambuie

Pour over rocks. Stir and serve.

RED BEER

Beer Mug
2-3 ounces tomato juice in mug

Fill with beer, stir gently. Add tabasco sauce if desired.

SALTY DOG

8 ounce glass
1½ ounce vodka
3 ounces grapefruit juice
1 teaspoon lemon juice

Pour over rocks, sprinkle with salt and serve.

SCORPION

15 ounce glass
Mixing cup, 4 ounces ice
2 ounces light rum
2 ounces orange juice
½ ounce lemon juice
1 ounce brandy
½ ounce Orgeat syrup

Blend and strain. Add ice cubes to fill. Garnish with orange slice.

SAZERAC

5½ ounce glass
¼ teaspoon Absinthe
½ teaspoon sugar
¼ teaspoon bitters
2 ounces bourbon
1 teaspoon water

Mix, pour over ice cubes. Add twisted lemon peel.

SCOTCH AND MILK

8 ounce glass with ice
2 ounces Scotch
Fill with milk
1 teaspoon sugar

Shake and pour over ice.

SIDE CAR

5 ounce cocktail glass rimmed with sugar
Mixing cup with
4 ounces ice
1½ ounces lemon juice
½ ounce triple sec
1 ounce brandy

Blend and strain.

SINGAPORE SLING

11 ounce glass ½ full of ice
Mixing cup with crushed ice
1½ ounces lemon juice
½ ounce Grenadine
1 ounce gin

Blend and strain. Fill with soda. Pour ½ ounce cherry brandy on top. Garnish with cherry and orange slice.

SCREWDRIVER

8 ounce glass
¾ filled with ice
1 ounce vodka

Fill with orange juice.

SCOTCH MIST

5½ ounce glass
½ filled with crushed ice
1 ounce Scotch
¼ ounce Irish Mist

SILVER FIZZ

11 ounce glass ½ filled with ice
2 ounces lemon juice
1 teaspoon sugar
1 ounce gin
1 egg white

Blend and strain. Top with soda.

SLOE GIN FIZZ

11 ounce glass ¾ full of ice
Juice of half of lemon
1 teaspoon sugar
2 ounces Sloe Gin

Blend and pour. Fill with soda. Stir & garnish with cherry.

SLOE SCREW

8 ounce glass, ice
1 ounce Sloe Gin
½ ounce Southern Comfort

Fill to top with orange juice and stir.

SOMBRERO

8 ounce glass filled with ice
1 ounce coffee flavored brandy
Fill with milk

Stir and serve.

SOUTHERN COMFORT
MANHATTAN

5½ ounce glass, ¾ full of ice
1½ ounces Southern Comfort
¼ ounce dry vermouth

Stir and serve.

STINGER

5½ ounce glass, filled with ice
½ ounce Creme De Menthe
1½ ounces Brandy

Mix and Serve.

TAHITI CLUB

5½ ounce glass
Mixing cup with 4 ounces ice
2 ounces light rum
1 tablespoon lemon juice
1 tablespoon lime juice
1 tablespoon pineapple juice
1 tablespoon Grenadine

Blend and strain. Add slice of lemon.

TEQUILA SUNRISE

11 ounce glass, ½ full of ice
2 ounces tequila
4 ounces orange juice
½ ounce Grenadine

Stir tequila and orange juice. Pour into glass.
Pour Grenadine slowly allowing it to settle.
Stir. Garnish with lime.

TOM & JERRY

1 coffee mug
1 egg in mug beaten
1 teaspoon sugar
½ ounce rum
2 ounces brandy

Fill with hot milk. Sprinkle with nutmeg.

TOM COLLINS

11 ounce glass, ½ full of ice
2 ounces lemon juice
1½ ounces gin
1 teaspoon sugar

Fill with soda. Stir and garnish with orange slice and cherry. For John Collins substitute whiskey for gin.

VELVET HAMMER

5½ ounce glass
Mixing cup and ice
1 ounce vodka
½ ounce white Creme De Cacao
¾ ounce cream

Blend and strain into pre-chilled cocktail glass.

VESUVIUS

Cordial glass · 1 ounce
¾ ounce brown Creme De Cacao
¼ ounce Green Chartreuse

Pour Green Chartreuse over top. Light on fire. Allow glass to cool before serving.

VODKA COLLINS

Tall 11 ounce Collins glass ½ full of ice
2 ounces lemon juice
1½ ounce vodka
1 teaspoon sugar

Fill with soda. Stir; garnish with orange slice and cherry.

VODKA GIMLET

5½ ounce glass with ice
1½ ounces vodka
½ ounce Rose's lime juice

Garnish with slice of lime.

WARD EIGHT

8 ounce glass
Mixing cup with 4 ounces ice
Juice of ½ lemon
2 ounces whiskey
1 tablespoon sugar
1 teaspoon Grenadine

Blend and strain. Add slice of orange.

WATERMELON COOLER

11 ounce glass
Mixing cup with 3 ounces ice
½ cup watermelon juice
2 ounces rum
½ ounce lime juice
1 tablespoon maraschino liqueur
1 teaspoon sugar

Pour and add ice cubes to fill. Garnish with slice of lime.

WHISKEY SOUR

4½ ounce glass
Mixing cup with 3 ounces ice
Juice of ½ lemon
1 ounce whiskey
½ teaspoon sugar

Blend and strain. Garnish with cherry and orange slice. All other sours substitute liquor of choice in same proportions.

WHITE RUSSIAN

5½ ounce glass, ¾ full of ice
1½ ounces vodka
½ ounce Kahlua

Top with cream and stir.

WHITE SPIDER

5½ ounce glass, ½ full of ice
1 ounce white Creme De Cacao
1 ounce white Creme De Menthe
1 ounce vodka

Mix with crushed ice. Pour and serve.

WHITE WINE SPRITZER

11 ounce glass, ½ full of ice.
3 ounces white wine

Fill rest with soda water. Stir.

ZOMBIE

11 ounce glass
1 ounce pineapple juice
1 tablespoon
  Rose's lime juice
Juice of ½ orange
1 teaspoon sugar
½ ounce apricot brandy
2 ounces light rum
1 ounce dark rum
1 ounce Grenadine

Put in blender with crushed ice. Strain into glass. Garnish with orange slice and cherry. Carefully float ½ ounce of 150 proof rum on top.

ALCOHOL
STOCKING YOUR HOME BAR

TYPES OF LIQUOR TO HAVE:

1 CASE BEER
1 LITRE VODKA
1 LITRE BOURBON
1 LITRE CANADIAN WHISKEY
1 LITRE IRISH WHISKEY
1 LITRE BLENDED WHISKEY
1 LITRE GIN
1 LITRE TANQUERAY (Optional)
1 LITRE LIGHT RUM
1 LITRE DARK RUM
1 LITRE TEQUILA
1 PINT DRY VERMOUTH
1 PINT SWEET VERMOUTH
1 LITRE BRANDY
1 LITRE CREME DE CACAO (White)
1 PINT BENEDECTINE
½ GALLON WHITE WINE
½ GALLON ROSE
1 QUART PORT
1 PINT TRIPLE SEC
1 PINT KAHLUA
1 PINT AMARETTO
1 PINT GALLIANO
1-8 OZ. CAN PINEAPPLE JUICE
1 PINT CREME DE MENTHE
1 PINT IRISH MIST
3 PINTS ASSORTED LIQUEURS
  CREME DE NOYAUX

CREME DE BANANA
CREME DE ALMOND
GREEN CREME DE MENTHE
BLUE CURACAO
CHERRY HEERING
TUACA
CREME DE COCONUT
ABSINTHE
DRAMBUIE
SLOE GIN
1 PINT SOUTHERN COMFORT

STOCKING YOUR HOME BAR
MIXES AND MATCHES

2 QUARTS COKE
2 QUARTS 7-UP
2 QUARTS GINGER ALE
2 QUARTS CLUB SODA
1 QUART CAN TOMATO JUICE
½ GALLON ORANGE JUICE
2 QUARTS TONIC WATER
1 SMALL BOTTLE GRENADINE
1 BOTTLE ROSE'S LIME JUICE
1 SMALL BOTTLE WORCESTERSHIRE SAUCE
1 SMALL JAR INSTANT COFFEE
1 SMALL BOTTLE CONCENTRATED LEMON
    JUICE
1 SMALL BOTTLE ANGOSTURA BITTERS
1 SMALL JAR FILLED WITH SUGAR CUBES
2 LIMES
2 LEMONS

1 SMALL JAR MARASCHINO CHERRIES
SALT AND PEPPER SHAKERS
1 JAR OLIVES

BAR TOOLS

JIGGER
COCKTAIL SHAKER
MARTINI PITCHER
CAN OPENER (PIERCING TYPE)
CORKSCREW
BOTTLE CAP OPENER
MIXING SPOON, LONG HANDLED
MEASURING SPOONS
SHARP KNIFE
CUTTING BOARD
FRUIT JUICE SQUEEZER
ICE CUBE BUCKET
TONGS
BLENDER (ELECTRIC)
ICE CRUSHER
COASTERS
SWIZZLE STICKS

COMMON MEASUREMENTS

DASH . . . . 1/8 OUNCE
1/2 PINT . . . . 8 OUNCES
PINT . . . . 16 OUNCES
FIFTH . . . . 25.6 OUNCES
QUART . . . . 32 OUNCES
HALF GALLON . . . . 64 OUNCES
MAGNUM . . . . 52 OUNCES
QUARTER KEG . . . . 8 GALLONS
HALF BARREL . . . . 16 GALLONS
BARREL . . . . 32 GALLONS
ICE SCOOP . . . . 6 OUNCES

Punches (Containing Alcohol)

BANANA EUPHORIA BOWL
(24 servings)

10 medium size ripe bananas
1 cup lime juice
1¼ cup sugar
1 - 750 ML light rum
10 ounces 151 proof rum
1 quart plus 12 ounces pineapple juice
12 ounces mango nectar
3 limes sliced

Cut 8 bananas into thin slices and place in electric blender with lime juice and sugar. Blend well until smooth. Pour over block of ice in punch bowl. Add both kinds of rum, pineapple juice, and nectar. Stir well. Cut remaining bananas into thin slices. Cut lime into thin slices. Float both banana and lime slices on punch.

BLACKBERRY BRANDY PUNCH
(12 servings)

1 litre blackberry brandy
1 litre ginger ale
16 ounces 7-Up
2½ cups unsweetened pineapple juice
1 orange sliced
1 lemon sliced

In a large punch bowl, combine all ingredients excluding ginger ale and 7-Up. Place a large block of ice into punch bowl and stir. Add soda pop just before serving.

CHAMPAGNE PUNCH

1½ cups lemon juice
2/3 cups sugar
1½ quarts cranberry juice
6 litres champagne
2 litres ginger ale
1 cup brandy

Stir lemon juice and sugar together in a large kettle until sugar dissolves. Add cranberry juice. To serve, pour over large block of ice in large punch bowl. Add champagne, ginger ale and brandy. Mix gently. Serves 2 dozen.

CHERRY FRUIT PUNCH (24 servings)

3 quarts orange juice
3 cups lemon juice
1 cup Maraschino cherries (and liquid)
4 quarts sparkling white grape juice
1 litre gin
2 oranges sliced

Add your gin with your fruit mixture, allow to ripen. Mix orange and lemon juice with the cherries. Put a large block of ice into large punch bowl. Add fruit mixture, then pour in grape juice. Garnish with the orange slices.

COGNAC AND RUM PUNCH
(24 servings)

2 - 10½ ounce packages frozen sliced peaches
1 litre dark rum
1 - 750 ML cognac
2 cups lemon Juice
2 cups lime juice
2 cups sugar
1 litre club soda

Allow peaches to thaw at room temperature. Place in blender and blend for 1 minute at high speed. Add rum, cognac, juices and sugar. Stir until sugar dissolves. Allow punch to ripen in refrigerator for about 1 hour. Pour over large block of ice in punch bowl. Pour in club soda just before serving.

CRANBERRY GIN PUNCH (12 servings)

46 ounce bottle cranberry juice cocktail
   (chilled)
6 ounce can frozen orange juice
1 litre gin
1 litre 7-Up
1 orange sliced

In large punch bowl, place juices and gin. Stir well. Place a large block of ice into punch bowl. Add 7-Up just before serving. Garnish with orange slices.

DAIQUIRI PUNCH (12 servings)

1½ quarts cracked ice
12 ounce can limeade (concentrate)
1 - 750 ML light rum

Place ice in large punch bowl. Add limeade and rum. Stir well. Strain into cocktail glasses and serve at once.

EGGNOG (12 servings)

4 egg yolks
2/3 cups sugar
2 quarts milk (scalded), allow to cool
1 teaspoon vanilla extract
1 teaspoon cinnamon
4 egg whites
4 tablespoons sugar
1 - 500 ML whiskey

Beat sugar into egg yolks. Slowly stir in milk. Cook in double boiler over hot (not boiling) water, stirring constantly until mixture coats spoon. Cool, add vanilla and spices and whiskey. Beat egg whites until foamy. Gradually add 4 tablespoons sugar, beating until soft peaks form. Fold into punch bowl; chill 3-4 hours.

FESTIVE MILK PUNCH (24 servings)

3/4 cup sugar
1 litre whiskey
7 quarts milk
1/2 teaspoon nutmeg

Mix all ingredients in a large kettle. Pour over large block of ice in large punch bowl.

FISH HOUSE PUNCH (24 servings)

3 cups sugar
4 cups water
2 quarts lemon juice
1/2 litre dark rum
1/2 litre brandy
Lemon slices

Place sugar and water in large sauce pan. Heat and stir until sugar dissolves. Pour into large punch bowl, adding remaining ingredients. Allow to ripen for 2 hours at room temperature. Add a large block of ice and mix gently. Garnish with lemon slices.

GRAPEFRUIT GIN PUNCH (24 servings)

12 ounce can frozen grapefruit juice
12 ounce can frozen orange juice
1 litre gin
2 oranges sliced
12 Maraschino cherries
1/2 teaspoon ginger
2 litres ginger ale

In a large punch bowl, place fruit juices and liquor. Stir. Add the fruit and ginger. Place a large block of ice into bowl. Stir. Allow to ripen for 1 hour at room temperature. Add the ginger ale just before serving.

HOT GRAPE PUNCH

20 cinnamon sticks
2 quarts grape juice
1 quart boiling water
1/2 cup lemon juice
1 cup sugar
Whole nutmegs (cracked)
1 litre gin

Tie the spices in cheesecloth. Place the spice bag and above ingredients except for gin, in a large kettle (not aluminum) and simmer, uncovered, stirring occasionally 10-15 minutes, adding gin to taste (up to 1 litre) discard spice bag. Serve hot.

LUAU PUNCH (32 servings)

2 - 46 ounce cans unsweetened pineapple juice
2 quarts orange juice
1/2 can Creme De Coconut
2 cups lemon juice
2 cups sugar
1 litre dark rum
1 orange sliced
1 lemon sliced
2 medium bananas sliced thin
2 litres ginger ale

In large punch bowl, place fruit juices, sugar, fruit slices, and Creme De Coconut. Stir well until sugar is dissolved. Add rum. Place a large block of ice into bowl. Allow mixture to ripen at room temperature for 1 hour. Add ginger ale just before serving.

RHINE WINE PUNCH (24 servings)

2 quarts orange juice
1 litre rhine wine
1 litre light rum
2 cups sugar
1/2 cup lemon juice
2-3 oranges sliced

Mix juices, wine and rum. Taste before adding sugar, if necessary. Place a large block of ice in large punch bowl. Add mixture and stir well. Garnish with orange slices.

RASPBERRY DELIGHT

1 quart pineapple juice
1 litre ginger ale
1 quart pineapple sherbet
1 quart raspberry sherbet
1 litre rum

Blend the above ingredients together in a large punch bowl, stir until well blended. Add rum to taste. Serve chilled over crushed ice.

STRAWBERRIES VODKA PUNCH
(24 servings)

12 ounce can frozen lemonade (thawed)
12 ounce can frozen orange juice (thawed)
12 ounce can frozen limeade (thawed)
10½ ounce can frozen strawberries (thawed)
1 litre vodka
2 litres 7-Up

In large punch bowl, combine fruit juices and vodka. Stir well. Add thawed strawberries. Allow mixture to ripen at room temperature for about 1 hour. Place a large block of ice in punch bowl. Add 7-Up just before serving.

VODKA LIME PUNCH

2 - 12 ounce cans frozen limeade
1 litre vodka
6 limes sliced
2 litres 7-Up

In large punch bowl, place Lime-Ade and 7-Up. Stir well. Add vodka and lime slices. Place block of ice into punch bowl and allow to chill for 15 minutes. Serves 10.

WHISKEY CITRUS PUNCH (36 servings)

1 quart orange juice
2 cups lemon juice
2 cups lime juice
2 cups sugar
1/2 cup grenadine
2 lemons thinly sliced
2 limes thinly sliced
2 litres whiskey
1 litre club soda

Place fruit juices and sugar into a large punch bowl. Stir until sugar dissolves. Place a large block of ice into large punch bowl. Add the whiskey and the fruit slices. Allow to ripen in refrigerator for 1 hour. Right before serving, pour in the club soda.

WHISKEY FRUIT JUICE PUNCH
(24 servings)

1 litre whiskey
12 ounce can frozen lemonade
12 ounce can frozen orange juice
12 ounce can frozen limeade
2 litres 7-Up

In large punch bowl, place whiskey and fruit juices. Stir well. Place a large block of ice in punch bowl. Add the 7-Up just before serving. Makes about 2 dozen servings.

Non-Alcoholic Drinks

APRICOT SWIZZLE (7 servings)

2 cups cold water
1 12-ounce can chilled apricot nectar
1 6-ounce can frozen lemonade concentrate,
    thawed
1/4 cup sugar
2 tablespoons instant tea powder
Ice cubes
1 28-ounce bottle chilled ginger ale

Combine water, nectar, lemonade concentrate, sugar and tea powder; stir till sugar and tea dissolve. Pour over ice into 7 large glasses about 2/3 full. Slowly pour in ginger ale; stir gently to mix. Serve immediately.

BANANA COW (4 servings)

2 medium bananas
1 cup cold milk
2 tablespoons honey
1/4 teaspoon vanilla
5-6 ice cubes
lime wedges

Combine all ingredients excluding lime wedges into a blender. Blend at high speed until smooth. Pour into 4 tall glasses. Garnish with a lime wedge. Serve immediately.

BANANA MILK SHAKE (3 servings)

2 cups milk
2 ripe medium bananas
2 tablespoons sugar or molasses

Combine all ingredients in a blender. Blend at high speed for about 1 minute. Mixture should be smooth & foamy. Pour into glasses and serve immediately.

BANANA MOCHA SHAKE (4 servings)

2 or 3 medium bananas
2 cups cold coffee
1 pint vanilla ice cream
1 teaspoon vanilla extract
1/3 cup sugar
Maraschino cherries for garnish.

Combine all the ingredients excluding the garnish into a blender. Blend at one minute at medium speed. Serve in frosted mugs or glasses topped with a cherry.

CARAMEL MILK (1 serving)

1 cup hot milk
2 tablespoons dark brown sugar
1 dash of vanilla extract

Combine all the ingredients in a mug. Stir and serve warm.

CRANBERRY SODA (6 servings)

2 cups fresh cranberries, washed and
  stemmed
1 cup cold water
Dash of salt
1 cup sugar
1 pint vanilla ice cream
1 28-oz. bottle of chilled club soda
Colored straws for stirrers

1. Combine the cranberries, water, salt and sugar in a saucepan. Bring to a boil and reduce heat. Simmer until cranberries burst and are soft. Set aside to cool.
2. When ready to serve, place a spoonful of ice cream into each tall glass. Add 2 or 3 table-spoons of the cranberry mixture, and fill the glass with club soda. Add a straw and stir gently. Serve immediately.

CHOCO-ORANGE FLOAT (6 servings)

2 cups chilled orange juice
2 12-ounce cans chilled ginger ale
1 pint chocolate ice cream
Grated orange peel for garnish.

Divide the orange juice and ginger ale among 6 tall frosted glasses. Stir to blend, then top each with a spoonful of ice cream and a sprinkling of orange peel. Serve immediately.

COCONUT COCKTAIL (2 servings)

1/2 cup chilled orange juice
1/2 cup plain yogurt
1/2 cup cream of coconut
3/4 cup chilled club soda
Orange slices for garnish

Combine the orange juice, yogurt and cream of coconut in a blender, and blend at high speed for 1 minute. Place 1 or 2 ice cubes in 2 tall frosted glasses. Fill each glass half way with the mixture, then add the club soda. Garnish each glass with an orange slice and serve.

DISCO MANGO (2 servings)

1 cup chilled watermelon chunks
1/2 cup canned chilled mango nectar
1/4 cup chilled orange juice
Ice cubes

Place watermelon in a blender and blend until smooth. Add mango nectar, orange juice and blend just to mix. (Do not over blend.) Place a few ice cubes in each of two 8 ounce glasses. Pour mixture in equal amounts over ice cubes in glasses and serve immediately.

FRUIT COOLER (6 servings)

1 envelope unsweetened raspberry flavored
   soft drink mix
1/2 cup sugar
1 46-ounce can chilled unsweetened pineapple
   juice
1/2 cup chilled orange juice
1/4 cup chilled lemon juice
Ice cubes

Combine raspberry-flavored soft drink mix, sugar and pineapple juice. Stir to dissolve. Add remaining fruit juices. Chill. Pour over ice into 6 glasses. Serve immediately.

FROSTY CRANBERRY COCKTAIL
(7 servings)

1 6-ounce can frozen cranberry juice cocktail
  concentrate
1 medium banana
2 tablespoons lemon juice
4 cups ice cubes

Combine cranberry juice, banana, and lemon juice into a blender. Cover; blend until smooth. Add 1/2 of the ice cubes; cover. Blend till smooth. Add remaining ice cubes. Cover; blend till slushy. Pour into glasses. Garnish each with a banana slice if desired. Serve immediately.

FRESH PEACH SHAKE (2 servings)

1 cup diced fresh peaches
1 to 2 tablespoons sugar
2 tablespoons lemon juice
1 cup cold milk
1/2 pint vanilla ice cream

Combine all ingredients in a blender. Blend at medium to high speed until smooth and fluffy. Pour into 2 large glasses. Serve immediately.

GINGER MINT (1 serving)

1 whole fresh lime
Ginger ale, chilled
Sprigs of fresh mint for garnish.

Squeeze fresh lime juice into a tall frosted glass. Add some ice cubes and fill with ginger ale. Stir; and add the mint.

HOMEMADE CRANBERRY JUICE
(4 servings)

1 pound washed fresh cranberries
2 cups of sugar
6 cups of water

Combine the cranberries, sugar and water in a 2 quart saucepan and bring to boil. Reduce heat and simmer until the cranberries burst and are soft. Place a sieve over a large bowl and line it with cheesecloth. Strain the cranberry juice through the cheesecloth. Cool and serve over ice, or refrigerate and use as needed.

HOT MULLED CIDER

3/4 cup brown sugar
1/4 teaspoon salt
1 teaspoon ground cloves
4 cinnamon sticks
2 dashes nutmeg
1/2 gallon apple cider

Combine ingredients in a heavy sauce pan. Slowly bring to a boil and simmer about 20 minutes. Remove cinnamon sticks. Serve hot garnished with orange slices. Serves 10.

LEMON COFFEE (2 servings)

2 cups cold, strong black coffee
1 cup lemon sherbet, slightly softened
1 tablespoon grated lemon rind
1 tablespoon lemon juice
2 tablespoons sugar
Maraschino cherries for garnish

Combine all the ingredients excluding the garnish into a blender. Blend at medium speed for about 2 minutes. Serve in frosted glasses, garnished with a cherry. Serve immediately.

MORNING SUN SHAKE
(3 servings)

1 cup orange sherbet
1½ cup cold milk
1½ cup chilled apricot nectar

Combine all ingredients in a blender. Blend at high speed until smooth. Serve immediately.

MOCK CHAMPAGNE (1 serving)

1 sugar cube
2 dashes Angostura bitters
Chilled club soda

Place the sugar cube in the center of a chilled champagne glass. Pour the Angostura bitters over the ice cube and allow the cube to dissolve a little. Pour in the club soda to fill the champagne glass. Serve.

MOCHA DELIGHT (2 servings)

1 square unsweetened chocolate coarsely
  chopped.
1/4 cup boiling water
1 tablespoon instant coffee
1 tablespoon sugar
1½ cups milk
Whipped cream and chocolate shavings for
  garnish

Combine all the ingredients excluding the garnish in a blender and blend at high speed for 30 seconds. Pour into 2 tall glasses and top with a spoonful of whipped cream and some chocolate shavings. Serve.

MILLIE'S SPICED ICE COFFEE
(4 servings)

1 cinnamon stick
4 whole cloves
6 tablespoons sugar
4 cups strong hot coffee
Vanilla ice cream or heavy cream for garnish

Combine the spices and sugar with the coffee. Stir and allow to cool to room temperature. Pour into a glass pitcher and chill for a few hours in the refrigerator. Remove the spices and pour ice coffee in 4 tall glasses with a bit of ice cream or heavy cream mixed in. Serve immediately.

NATURE'S OWN SUN KISSED TEA
(12 servings)

3 quarts cold water
8 tea bags
Sugar and lemon to taste
Fresh mint sprigs for garnish

Combine the cold water and tea bags in a large pot and set it in a sunny spot for most of the day. At dinner time, remove the tea bags and add the sugar and lemon to taste. Serve over ice with a mint sprig in each glass.

OLD FASHIONED
CHOCOLATE SODA (1 serving)

2 tablespoons chocolate syrup
1/4 cup cold milk
2 or 3 scoops vanilla ice cream
1 teaspoon vanilla extract
1 cup chilled club soda
Whipped cream & maraschino cherry for
   garnish.

Combine chocolate syrup, milk, 1 scoop
vanilla ice cream and vanilla extract in a tall
glass. Stir vigorously with a spoon to blend.
Fill a tall glass 2/3 full with club soda; stir. Add
1 or 2 more scoops of ice cream; fill glass with
club soda. Garnish with whipped cream and
cherry. Serve immediately.

ORANGE FIZZLE (4 servings)

1 6-ounce can frozen orange juice, thawed
1 28-ounce bottle chilled ginger ale
Orange slices and maraschino cherries for
   garnish

Fill 4 tall glasses with ice cubes. Place a heaping tablespoon of orange juice concentrate in
each glass, and fill with ginger ale. Stir to blend
thoroughly. Top with orange slices and cherries, and serve immediately.

ORANGE ICE CREAM SODA (6 servings)

**1 12-ounce can frozen orange juice concen-
trate, thawed.
1/2 cup light cream
1 28-ounce bottle chilled ginger ale
1 pint vanilla ice cream
1 pint orange sherbet**

Put a heaping tablespoon of orange juice concentrate into each glass. Add 1 tablespoon of
light cream and mix well. Stir in 1/4 cup of
ginger ale, and add 1 scoop each of the ice
cream and the sherbet. Fill the glasses with the
remaining ginger ale. Stir gently and serve with
a straw and a long handled spoon.

ORANGE JULIUS (4 servings)

**1/2 of a 6-ounce can frozen orange juice con-
centrate
1/2 teaspoon vanilla extract
1/2 cup cold milk
1/4 cup sugar
1/2 cup cold water
5-6 ice cubes.**

Combine all ingredients in a blender. Blend at
high speed until smooth & frothy. Serve immediately.

ORANGE STRAWBERRY REFRESHER (8 servings)

2 cups orange juice
1 quart apple juice
1 pint strawberry sherbet
Orange peel for garnish

Pour orange juice and apple juice into a large pitcher and stir well. Fill tall frosted glasses with cracked ice and add the juice. Top each glass with a scoop of sherbet, garnish with an orange peel. Serve 8 glasses immediately.

POKER PLAYERS SHAKE (4 servings)

2 tablespoons powdered instant coffee
Pinch of salt
1/4 cup sugar
1 quart cold milk
1/4 teaspoon peppermint extract
2 pints vanilla ice cream
Maraschino cherries for garnish

Combine the instant coffee, salt and sugar in a large pitcher. Add 1 cup of the milk and stir until the coffee and sugar are dissolved. Add the remaining milk and the peppermint extract and stir well. Pour into soda glasses, top each with a scoop of ice cream, and a maraschino cherry. Add a straw and a long handled spoon. Serve.

PEPPERMINT FLUFF (4 servings)

3 cups cold milk
3/4 cups crushed pineapple candy
1/4 cup cold water
1½ teaspoons lemon juice
1/2 teaspoon vanilla extract
1/4 cup dry milk
1 tablespoon sugar

Scald milk in double boiler. Add candy and stir until dissolved. Chill. Combine water, lemon juice, vanilla, and dry milk in a deep bowl. Beat with electric beater about 6 minutes or until stiff. Gradually add sugar. Beat 1 minute or until blended. Chill. When ready to serve, whip peppermint mixture until foamy. Fold in half of whipped dry milk mixture. Pour into glasses. Use remaining whipped dry milk to top each drink about 1/4 cup per glass. Sprinkle with bits of crushed peppermint candy. Serve immediately.

PEACH ALMOND COOLER (4 servings)

2 cups cold milk
1 cup chilled canned sliced peaches with syrup
1 cup peach yogurt
1/4 teaspoon almond extract

Combine all ingredients in a blender. Blend at high speed for about 1 minute until smooth. Serve immediately in chilled glasses.

PINEAPPLE MILK SHAKE (1 serving)

1 cup cold milk
1/2 cup crushed pineapple, undrained
1 teaspoon sugar
1 tablespoon lemon juice

Combine all ingredients into a blender. Blend at high speed for about 1 minute. Mixture should be smooth and foamy. Pour into a large chilled glass. Serve immediately.

PRAIRIE OYSTER (1 serving)

"Guaranteed to cure a hangover"
1 egg yolk
1 teaspoon Worcestershire sauce
2 dashes white vinegar
2 dashes Tabasco sauce
1 dash of salt
1 dash of pepper

Place the unbroken egg yolk in a champagne glass and add the remaining ingredients. Down the hatch!

PEPPERMINT MILK SHAKE (6 servings)

"A great way to salvage broken candy canes"
1/2 crushed peppermint candy
2 cups cold milk
1½ pints vanilla ice cream

Combine candy and milk in a blender. blend at medium speed for about 1 minute. Add the ice cream and blend until smooth. Pour into 6 6-ounce glasses. Serve immediately.

RASPBERRY ANGEL (1 serving)

1/2 cup chilled fresh red raspberries
2 tablespoons yogurt
2 tablespoons chilled club soda
2 teaspoons sugar

Combine all ingredients in a blender and blend until smooth. Strain into a 6-ounce glass. Place in freezer to thoroughly chill. Serve when chilled; do not add ice.

SHIRLEY TEMPLE

11 ounce glass
4 ounce lemon juice
1 ounce Grenadine
Fill with 7-Up

Add ice and garnish with cherry & orange slice.

SUMMER MADNESS (8 servings)

2 cups chilled orange juice
1 pint chocolate ice cream
1 28-ounce bottle chilled ginger ale
Grated orange peel and maraschino cherries
    for garnish.

Combine the orange juice and ice cream in a blender. Blend at medium speed for 30 seconds or until smooth. Fill glasses 3/4 full with crushed ice. Fill each glass, 1/2 way with ginger ale, then add the blender mixture, stirring gently. Garnish with the grated orange peel and a maraschino cherry. Serve.

SPARKLING QUICK ICE TEA
(6 servings)

6 tea bags
3 cups boiling water
1 litre 7-Up
Lemon, lime or orange slices for garnish

Combine the tea bags and boiling water in a teapot. Stir and allow to steep for 5 minutes. Pour tea into a large pitcher and chill. When ready to serve, stir in 7-Up. Serve over ice cubes in tall glasses garnished with a fruit slice.

TOMATO CLAM JUICE
PICKER-UPPER (1 serving)

1/4 cup chilled clam juice
1/2 cup chilled tomato juice
1/4 teaspoon horseradish
1/8 teaspoon celery salt
2 ice cubes

Combine all ingredients excluding the ice cubes in a blender. Blend at high speed for 30 seconds. Pour over ice cubes in an 8-ounce glass and serve.

TROPICAL COOLER (1 serving)

1 medium ripe banana
3/4 cup cold milk
1/4 cup chilled pineapple juice

Combine all ingredients in a blender. Blend at medium to high speed until smooth. Pour into a tall glass. Serve immediately.

THE DRY EDITH (1 serving)

"Try this if your stomach feels bloated after a festive holiday party."

1 large glass of club soda, with ice
1 large dash of Angostura bitters
1 large lemon peel

Add the bitters to the ice club soda. Garnish with a lemon peel and stir.

TOMATO PINEAPPLE GLOW (1 serving)

3 ounce chilled tomato juice
3 ounce chilled unsweetened pineapple juice
1 or 2 dashes of Tabasco sauce
1 pinch dried dill weed
1 pinch dried oregano
2 ice cubes
Celery stalk and parsley for garnish

Combine all ingredients excluding garnish and ice in a blender. Blend until mixed. Pour mixture into an 8 ounce glass and refrigerate for about 10 minutes to allow flavors to mature. Strain to remove herbs if desired. Add ice cubes and stir. Garnish with celery stalk and parsley. Serve.

THE PINK SNOWMAN (2 servings)

Serve in goblets or tall soda glasses
1 cup chilled orange juice
1 10-ounce package frozen strawberries, partially thawed.
1/2 cups cold water
2 large scoops vanilla ice cream
Strawberries or orange slices for garnish

Combine the juice, berries and water in a blender. Blend at medium speed for 30 seconds. Pour into tall glasses or goblets and add a scoop of ice cream to each. Garnish with fruit and serve immediately.

TOMATO ZINGER (1 serving)

1 cup chilled tomato juice
1 tablespoon fresh unstrained lemon juice
1/2 teaspoon Worcestershire sauce
3 squirts Tabasco sauce
1 pinch of salt
1 pinch black pepper

Combine all ingredients in a blender. Blend at high speed for 30 seconds. Pour over ice in an 8 ounce glass.

ZIPPY TOMATO JUICE COCKTAIL
(1 serving)

3/4 cup chilled tomato juice
1 teaspoon horseradish
1 dash of Tabasco sauce
1 dash of Worcestershire sauce
1 dash of lemon juice
Salt & pepper to taste
Lemon peel for garnish

Combine all the ingredients excluding the garnish in a short fat glass. Stir briskly. Add some ice and the lemon peel. Serve.

THE PINK DUMBO (1 Brandy Snifter)
"A Tasty Way to Toast the New Year"

1 teaspoon lime juice (fresh or bottled)
1 teaspoon grenadine
1 teaspoon sugar
½ cup bitter lemon
½ cup chilled unsweetened pink grapefruit juice

Combine lime juice, grenadine and sugar together in a snifter. Add ice cubes, bitter lemon and grapefruit juice. Stir and serve.

TEDDY BEAR GRAPEFRUIT (2 Servings)

⅓ cup honey
1 cup chilled grapefruit juice
1 cup cold milk
½ medium banana

Combine all ingredients in a blender. Blend at high speed until smooth. Serve immediately.

Punches (Non-Alcoholic)

APPLE PUNCH

3 quarts apple juice
4 cinnamon sticks
1 teaspoon ground cloves
1½ pints pineapple juice
1 cup lemon juice
1 quart orange juice
2 litres ginger ale

Place apple juice and spices in heavy sauce pan. Simmer uncovered for 15 minutes, mix the spiced juice with remaining fruit juices. To serve, place a large block of ice in a large punch bowl. Add the ginger ale. Serves 2 dozen.

CRANBERRY PUNCH

1 6-ounce can frozen orange juice concentrate, thawed
1 6-ounce can frozen pink lemonade concentrate, thawed
1 6-ounce can frozen pineapple juice concentrate, thawed
5 cups cold water
6 cups cranberry juice cocktail
1 litre chilled ginger ale

Combine all ingredients excluding ginger ale in a large punch bowl. Add ginger ale just before serving. Add a block of ice. Serve.

CITRUS PUNCH (40 servings)

1 6-ounce can frozen orange juice concentrate, thawed
1 6-ounce can frozen lemonade concentrate, thawed
1 6-ounce can frozen limeade concentrate, thawed
1 46-oz. can chilled pineapple juice
2 litres chilled ginger ale
Orange, lemon, and lime slices for garnish.

Combine all the fruit juices in a large punch bowl. Stir well. Just before serving add the ginger ale and a block of ice. Float the fruit slices on top. Serve.

FRUIT MEDLEY (for 50 people)

3 pounds sugar
1 gallon cold water
1/2 gallon crushed canned pineapple
1 46-ounce can unsweetened grapefruit juice
1 quart lemon juice (made from concentrate)
3 quarts orange juice
1/4 cup grated lemon peel
1/4 cup grated orange peel
1½ tablespoons whole cloves
10 cinnamon sticks
2 tablespoons allspice
4 cups strong, hot tea
Orange & lemon slices for garnish.

Combine the sugar and water in a large kettle. Bring to a boil, reduce the heat and simmer for 5-8 minutes. Set aside to cool. Strain the pineapple and place it and the fruit juices In a large punch bowl. Add the sugar-water mixture and the lemon and orange peel. Mix well. Add the spices to the hot tea and allow to steep for 15 minutes. Strain the tea & pour into the punch bowl. Just before serving, add a large block of ice and garnish with the lemon & orange slices.

GRAPE PUNCH (24 servings)

1 12-oz. can frozen grape juice concentrate, prepared according to instructions on the can
1 46-oz. can chilled Hawaiian Punch
1 litre chilled ginger ale

Pour the fruit juices into a large punch bowl. Stir well. Just before serving, add the ginger ale. Place a block of ice or an ice ring into the punch. Serve.

GUAVA FRUIT PUNCH (18 servings)

2 cups guava juice
1½ cups unsweetened pineapple juice
1 cup orange juice
3/4 cup lemon juice
1/2 cup sugar
3 tablespoons grenadine syrup
1 litre chilled ginger ale
Assorted fresh fruit for garnish

Combine all ingredients in a large punch bowl excluding ginger ale; stir until sugar is dissolved. Just before serving, add ginger ale. Add a block of ice or ice ring. Garnish with fresh fruit. Serve.

HOLIDAY FRUIT PUNCH (24 servings)

2 32-ounce bottles of chilled apple juice
2 32-ounce bottles of chilled cranberry juice
1 cup lemon juice
1 16-ounce can pineapple chunks, drained for
  garnish

Combine all ingredients in a large punch bowl.
Add a block of ice and serve.

JUNE BUG PUNCH (40 servings)

6 cups extra strong chilled tea
2½ cups sugar
3 cups chilled orange juice
2 cups chilled unsweetened grapefruit juice
1/2 cup lime juice
1/2 cup lemon juice
2 quarts chilled ginger ale
Garnish: fresh mint & lemon slices

Combine all the ingredients excluding the garnish in a large punch bowl. Stir well. Just before serving, add the ginger ale. Add an ice block and the garnish. Serve.

LOUISIANA LEMONADE (36 servings)

2 cups sugar
3 quarts chilled water
juice of 12 lemons, strained
1 pineapple, freshly sliced and juiced in a
    blender
2 quarts chilled club soda
Garnish: lemon slices, pineapple slices, fresh
    ripe strawberries

Combine sugar, water, lemon juice and pineapple juice into a large punch bowl. Mix well. When you are ready to serve, add the club soda. Stir gently. Add a block of ice. Add the garnish. Serve.

NON-ALCOHOLIC WASSAIL PUNCH (40 servings)

1 gallon apple cider
1 quart pineapple juice
1 quart orange juice
1 quart cranberry juice
1 tablespoon lemon juice
1/4 cup brown sugar
2 cinnamon sticks
8 whole cloves
1 teaspoon Angostura bitters
Orange slices for garnish

Combine all ingredients in a large kettle. Simmer 30 to 45 minutes. Add orange slices. Serve hot.

ORANGE SHERBET PUNCH
(12-15 servings)

1/2 gallon orange sherbet
2 quarts orange juice
2 litres orange soda pop

Put sherbet into large punch bowl. Add equal amounts of orange juice and soda pop. Garnish with orange slices.

QUICK AND EASY PUNCH
(12-15 servings)

1/2 gallon lime sherbet
1 can Hi-C "Citrus" drink
2 litres 7-Up

Put sherbet into a large punch bowl. Add equal amounts of the liquid, pouring slowly down the side of the bowl. Ladle into punch cups.

RASPBERRY FIZZLE (10 servings)

1/2 gallon raspberry sherbet
1 quart cranberry juice
1 quart orange juice
1 litre ginger ale
1 pint fresh raspberries

Put sherbet into a large punch bowl. Add the juices and fresh raspberries. Add the ginger ale. Ladle into punch cups.

ROSE GARDEN PUNCH (18 servings)

1 6-ounce can frozen lemonade concentrate,
  thawed
1 6-ounce can frozen orange juice concentrate,
  thawed
1 litre ginger ale
1 pint white catawba grape juice, chilled
2 6-ounce cans of water

Combine all ingredients in a large punch bowl.
Add a frozen ice ring & serve.

RASPBERRY FLOAT (20 servings)

3 3-ounce packages raspberry Jello
4 cups boiling water
1½ cups of sugar
4 cups cold water
1/2 cup lime juice
2½ cups orange juice
1½ cups lemon juice
1 litre chilled ginger ale
2 10-ounce packages frozen raspberries

Dissolve the Jello in boiling water; add sugar, cold water and juices. Cool, but do not chill. When ready to serve, pour punch into large punch bowl. Add frozen raspberries and stir until they break apart and are partially thawed. Add the ginger ale and a block of ice. Serve.

STRAWBERRY PUNCH (18 servings)

1 10-ounce package frozen strawberries, partially thawed
3 6-ounce cans frozen lemonade concentrate thawed
3 6-ounce cans water
1 litre chilled ginger ale

Whirl strawberries in a blender. Add lemonade & water, whirl again. Pour again into a large punch bowl. Add the ginger ale and a block of ice. Serve.

Personal Best Section

PERSONAL DRINK RECIPES

PERSONAL DRINK RECIPES

PERSONAL DRINK RECIPES

PERSONAL DRINK RECIPES

PERSONAL DRINK RECIPES

PERSONAL DRINK RECIPES

PERSONAL DRINK RECIPES

PERSONAL DRINK RECIPES

PERSONAL DRINK RECIPES

PERSONAL DRINK RECIPES

PERSONAL DRINK RECIPES

PERSONAL DRINK RECIPES

PERSONAL DRINK RECIPES

PERSONAL DRINK RECIPES